CODE
EXTRA

Trapped in the Tower

Jan Burchett and Sara Vogler • Jonatronix

Dragon Quest

OXFORD
UNIVERSITY PRESS

CODE Control Update:

My name is **CODE**. I am the computer that controls **Micro World**. **Team X** and **Mini** are trying to get the **CODE keys** and rescue **Macro Marvel**. My **BITEs** must stop them!

Team X are in: Dragon Quest zone

Team X

Mini

CODE key

BITE

Dragon Quest cameras

CAMERA 1 ● REC

Tiger sees a dragon to fight.

CAMERA 2 ● REC

He needs Cat to help him in her Bee-machine.

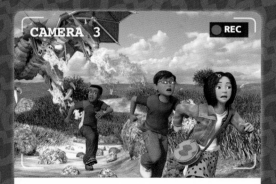

CAMERA 3 ● REC

The Dragon-BITE attacks Max, Ant and Mini.

CAMERA 4 ● REC

Max fights the BITE.

Status: The BITE has hurt its wing. Cat and Tiger are looking for the BITE.

Before you read

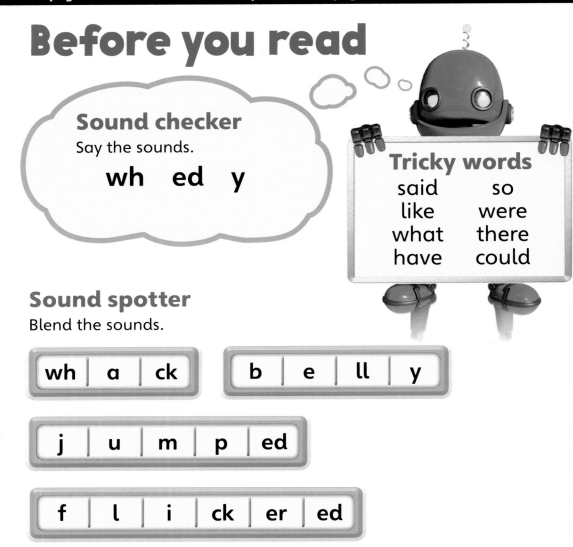

Sound checker

Say the sounds.

wh   ed   y

Tricky words

said	so
like	were
what	there
have	could

Sound spotter

Blend the sounds.

wh	a	ck

b	e	ll	y

j	u	m	p	ed

f	l	i	ck	er	ed

Into the zone

Do you think the BITE will try
to attack Team X again?

Cat and Tiger were looking for the Dragon-BITE.
"We might see it from that tower," said Cat.

They jumped from the jeep and went up the steps of the tower. Suddenly, Tiger's watch flashed.

"Wait a moment," whispered Tiger. "It looks like the BITE could be up there! Look out!"

CRASH!

The tower shuddered.

"It is the BITE," yelled Tiger.

"But it's not on top of the tower. We have been trapped!"

The BITE whacked the tower with its tail.

whack!

Fire flickered up the steps.
Even the MITEs wanted to flee.

What's the plan?

"There is one thing that could help us get down," said Cat.

"Yes! Let's get a lift with a dragon," said Tiger.
He aimed his cord at a dragon.

The cord missed the dragon's belly but hit its claws.
The dragon whisked Cat and Tiger off the tower.

"That was so lucky," said Cat. "We got out just in time."

"Just in time to train a dragon!"
said Tiger.

Now you have read ...
Trapped in the Tower

Text checker
Match each of these words from the story with the correct definition:

whispered	whacked	flickered	flee

- the flames of the fire flared up and died down again
- hit very hard
- run away to escape from danger
- spoke very softly

Look for each word in the story to check that it makes sense.

MITE fun
What do you think Cat and Tiger are thinking?

Would *you* like to fly with a dragon?